BRAZIL

Nicola Barber

FRANKLIN WATTS
LONDON • SYDNEY

First published in 2010 by Franklin Watts

© 2010 Arcturus Publishing Limited

Franklin Watts
338 Euston Road
London NW1 3BH

Franklin Watts Australia
Level 17/207 Kent Street, Sydney, NSW 2000

Produced by Arcturus Publishing Limited,
26/27 Bickels Yard, 151–153 Bermondsey Street, London SE1 3HA

The right of Nicola Barber to be identified as the author of this work has been asserted
by her in accordance with the Copyright, Designs and Patents Act 1988.

Series concept: Alex Woolf
Editor: Jacqueline McCann
Designer: Ian Winton
Maps and charts: Stefan Chabluk
Picture research: Jacqueline McCann and Shelley Noronha

Picture credits:
Agencia Estado Brazil: 22 (Alex Silva). Art Archive: 11 (Musée de la Marine Paris/Gianni Dagli Orti), 13 (Museu Historico
Nacional Rio de Janeiro Brazil/Gianni Dagli Orti). Corbis: cover right (James Davis), 3 (Gavin Heller), 6 (Frans Lanting),
8 (Andrew Hay), 9 (Fernando Soutello), 10 (Pierre Colombel), 12 (Art Archive/Alfredo Dagli Orti), 14 (Bettman),
24 (Reuters), 25 (Leo La Valle), 26 (Julia Waterlow), 28 (Paulo Whitaker/Reuters), 29 (Paulo Fridman), 30 (Bertrand
Gardel), 31 (Paulo Fridman), 36 (Frans Lanting), 37 (Paulo Whitaker), 39 (Jorge Adorno), 40 (Michael Reynolds),
41 (Eduardo Munoz). EASI-Images/The Discovery Photo Library: 34, 35 (Ed Parker). Getty: cover left (John Maler Jr),
15 (Dmitri Kessel), 16 (Antonio Scorza), 18 (SambaPhoto/Paulo Fridman), 19 (Evaristo Sa), 32 (Jose de Paula Machado),
33 (Paul Edmonson), 38 (Superstudio), 43 (Vanderlei Almeida). Still Pictures: 17 (Nigel Dickinson), 23 (Gabriel
Fernando), 42 (John Maier). TopFoto: 20, 21 (John Maier/The Image Works).

Cover captions:
Left: An elder from the Mebengokre Indians, also called the Kayapo, from Brazil. The traditional
headdress is made of feathers from the macaw and stork, both of which are endangered in Brazil.
Right: The modern government buildings in Brasília, designed by Oscar Niemeyer.

Every attempt has been made to clear copyright. Should there be any inadvertent omission,
please apply to the publisher for rectification.

A CIP catalogue record for this book is available from the British Library.

Dewey Decimal Classification Number: 981'.065

ISBN 978 0 7496 9530 9

Printed in China

Franklin Watts is a division of Hachette Children's Books, an Hachette Livre UK company.
www.hachettelivre.co.uk

Contents

CHAPTER 1

Introduction

Brazil is the world's fifth largest country, covering nearly half of the South American landmass. The eastern side of the country is entirely coastline, extending 7,367 km along the Atlantic Ocean. Brazil shares a border with every South American country except Ecuador and Chile. This massive nation, which is bigger than all of the countries in western Europe put together, has the highest levels of biodiversity (variety of life) of any region in the world. It is home to an amazing 15 to 20 per cent of all known species. These live in habitats that include rainforest, wetlands, savannah grassland (called *cerrado*) and coastal areas.

Amazonia

The Amazon river, which flows across northern Brazil, has the largest drainage basin in the world. The river has its origins high in the Andes mountains in Peru, to the west of Brazil. So much water flows through this huge river system that, at the river's mouth on Brazil's Atlantic coast, the fresh water dilutes the salty seawater more than 160 km from the shore. The Amazon basin is home to the largest rainforest region on Earth. Almost half of Brazil – more than 4 million sq km – is covered by rainforest. This means that Brazil has about one-third of the world's rainforest within its borders. The amount of rainforest that has been destroyed in recent decades is a major environmental issue.

Atlantic rainforest

Brazil has another type of rainforest along its Atlantic coastline. Known as Atlantic rainforest, it

This photograph shows the dramatic scenery of the Serra dos Órgãos National Park near Rio de Janeiro, the third national park created in Brazil. It was established in 1939 to protect the Atlantic rainforest that covers the hillsides.

Key
- ○ Cities over 1 million people
- ● Cities below 1 million people
- △ Mountain

once stretched in an unbroken band from Rio Grande do Norte at the easternmost tip of Brazil to Rio Grande do Sul in the south. Today, the rainforest survives only in fragments, but it remains home to vast numbers of plant and animal species, many of which are endangered.

Cerrado, caatinga and the Pantanal

South of the Amazon basin lies an area of highlands called the Planalto Brasileiro (Central Plateau). This broad plain is bisected by rivers, and is covered in *cerrado*, although large areas

With a maximum width of 4,319 km and length of 4,394 km, Brazil is almost as wide as it is long. It lies between the equator and the tropic of Capricorn and has a humid tropical and subtropical climate.

have been developed for agriculture. To the northeast, only hardy thorny shrubs and cacti can survive on the *sertão* (dry plains). This vegetation is known as *caatinga*. West of the Planalto Brasileiro is an area of wetland called the Pantanal. This vast swamp, which is about half the size of France, teems with wildlife.

A multicultural society

When Europeans first arrived in South America in 1500, the land that we now call Brazil was home to between two and six million native Indian people. Today an estimated 350,000 Indians live in Brazil, belonging to roughly 200 different tribes. Brazil was settled in the sixteenth century by Portuguese explorers who found that sugar cane grew well in the tropical climate. The Portuguese brought slaves from Africa to work on their sugar plantations. The different races intermingled and today many Brazilians are *mestiço* (mixed race) with ancestors from one of three main groups; Indian, white European (mostly Portuguese) and black African.

Immigrants from Italy arrived in the late nineteenth century, and from Germany in the early years of the twentieth century. There was a large influx of Japanese immigrants in the

BRAZIL'S POPULATION

White 53.7%
Mixed white and black 38.5%
Black 6.2%
Other (includes Japanese, Arab, Amerindian) 0.9%
Unspecified 0.7%

Source: CIA World Factbook, 2000 census

twentieth century, and today Brazil has the largest population of people with Japanese ancestry outside Japan itself. Descendants of Italian, German and Japanese immigrants tend to live in the south of the country, while the northeast has the highest population of mixed race Afro-Brazilians. Most native peoples live in the Amazon rainforest; the largest tribes include the Tikuna, the Guaraní and the Yanomami.

Despite being a multicultural society, race discrimination is a problem in Brazil. The ways of

A Guaraní family ride on a horse-drawn cart in southern Brazil. There are around 46,000 Guaraní people living in Brazil today.

life of Brazil's native peoples remain under threat from development of the Amazon rainforest. More than 60 per cent of the Afro-Brazilian population lives in poverty, and there are few black representatives in the worlds of Brazilian politics and business. Meanwhile, the richest 10 per cent of the population is almost exclusively white.

The Mardi Gras carnival is a major festival in Brazilian cities, particularly Rio de Janeiro. It is a multi-cultural event where Brazilians of all kinds come together.

Language and religion

Portuguese is the official language of Brazil. Brazil's native peoples speak many different languages, which belong to four main groups: Tupi, Arawak, Carib and Gê. Other languages, including Italian, German and Japanese, are also spoken by descendants of immigrants from these countries. Brazil is mainly a Roman Catholic country, with about two-thirds of the population calling themselves Catholics. There is also a strong Protestant Evangelical movement. Brazil has several religions that blend elements of

Christianity with beliefs brought by black slaves from Africa. One example is Candomblé, which is particularly strong in Bahia in the northeast.

CASE STUDY: CANDOMBLÉ

Candomblé is an African-Brazilian religion that is a mixture of the Catholic faith with Yoruba, Fon and Bantu beliefs. Candomblé means 'dance in honour of the gods'. Followers of Candomblé were persecuted for their beliefs until the 1970s, but the religion has grown in popularity since then. Followers believe in an all-powerful god called Oludumaré, who is attended by lesser gods. Some of these lesser gods, or *orixas*, provide a link between humans and the spirit world. Worship takes the form of dancing and singing.

CHAPTER 2

History

We know from archaeological evidence uncovered near the Amazonian towns of Santarém and Monte Alegre that Brazil's earliest inhabitants were established in the region at least 11,000 years ago. These early people were nomadic – they moved from place to place in search of food. Archaeologists have unearthed evidence including pottery, arrowheads and, in some coastal areas, large mounds of discarded shells which are the remains of the shellfish eaten by coastal peoples.

Terra da Vera Cruz

It is generally accepted that the Portuguese sailor Pedro Alvares Cabral 'discovered' Brazil for the Europeans. Cabral arrived in 1500 and was greeted by the Tupi Indians who inhabited the coastal regions at that time. The Portuguese stayed only long enough to christen the land *Terra da Vera Cruz* (Land of the True Cross). When they set sail again, they took with them logs from the brazilwood tree *(pau brasil)* from which they found they could extract a valuable red dye. It was from this wood that the country eventually got its name.

It was another 30 years before the Portuguese returned to settle in their newly claimed colony. Worried that other European nations were taking over the lucrative trade in brazilwood, the Portuguese king divided the colony into

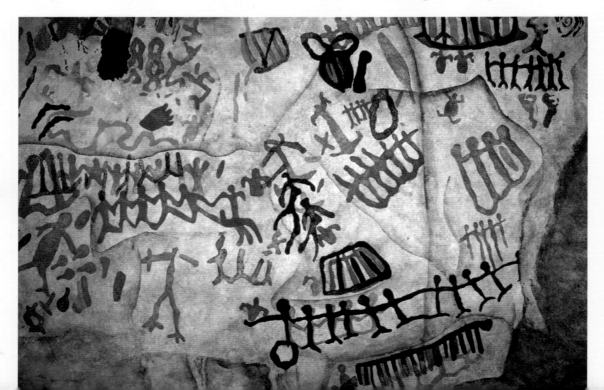

These prehistoric rock paintings, showing people with their hands and feet linked, date back to 3,000 BCE. They are found in Lapa do Dragão, in central Brazil.

Portuguese and French ships engaged in battle off the coast of Brazil in the sixteenth century. Both the French, and in the seventeenth century the Dutch, challenged Portugal for control of its new colony.

15 regions called captaincies, each under the control of a different Portuguese nobleman. However, only two of these were successful, and, in 1549, the king strengthened his control by sending a governor-general, Tomé de Sousa, to the colony. Sousa set up a capital at Salvador, which remained the country's capital until 1763, when Rio de Janeiro took over.

Sugar and slavery

The Portuguese set up sugar cane plantations to supply the lucrative European market for sugar. The settlers needed a workforce to cultivate the sugar, and they forced many Indians to work as slaves. However, the Indian population was falling dramatically. They had no immunity to diseases such as measles and smallpox that had been imported by the Europeans, and several epidemics wiped out tens of thousands of native people.

The Portuguese quickly turned to a more reliable source of slaves by importing captives from west Africa.

From about 1550, black slaves replaced the Indians as workers on the plantations. The conditions endured by the slaves were atrocious, and there were numerous revolts and uprisings. Some slaves set up free territories, called *quilombos*. By the time slavery was abolished in Brazil in 1888, about 3.6 million African slaves had been brought to the country – around 40 per cent of the total shipped to the Americas.

CASE STUDY: THE *QUILOMBOS*

Escaped slaves set up communities, or *quilombos*, all over Brazil. The most famous and longest-lasting was the Republic of Palmares, which existed from 1630 until 1695 when it was finally destroyed by government forces. Under their leader, Zumbi, the inhabitants of Palmares became skilled fighters as they defended their community against Portuguese attacks. Today, Zumbi is a national hero in Brazil.

Brazilian settlers relied on slaves brought from West Africa to provide a workforce. In this nineteenth century print, slaves are shown washing diamonds, watched by their taskmasters.

convert the native people to Christianity. They built missions in remote parts of Brazil, and tried to offer the Indians some protection.

In the 1690s, groups of *bandeirantes* discovered gold in the region north of São Paulo, known today as Minas Gerais. The find prompted a gold rush and thousands of Portuguese settlers came to Brazil. Many black slaves were sent to work in the gold mines. Towns sprung up overnight, and an area that had been virtually empty had a population of 500,000 by 1800.

The *bandeirantes*

During the seventeenth and eighteenth centuries, groups of adventurers known as *bandeirantes* explored deeper into the interior of Brazil. The *bandeirantes* plundered Indian villages and captured their inhabitants to sell as slaves. Thousands of Indians fled their native lands to escape these attacks. Some sought safety with Christian missionaries, called Jesuits. The Jesuits had been sent to Brazil by the king of Portugal to

The gold mines brought immense wealth to the region, and prompted the move of the colonial capital to Rio de Janeiro.

Independence

In 1807, the Portuguese royal family arrived in Brazil. The armies of the French emperor Napoleon I had invaded Portugal and were threatening its capital, Lisbon. The prince regent, Dom João, fell in love with Brazil. In 1815, he

CASE STUDY: TIRADENTES

Calls for independence from Portugal started during the seventeenth century, as wealthy settlers began to resent the Portuguese colonial government and its heavy taxes. The first major rebellion against Portuguese rule was led by a dentist called Joaquim José da Silva Xavier. He was better known by his nickname Tiradentes (tooth-puller). Tiradentes and his fellow conspirators were all arrested, and Tiradentes was executed. He rapidly became a national hero, and is still celebrated in Brazil today.

increasingly powerful. However, just as on the sugar plantations, the cultivation of coffee relied on slave labour. Despite increasing pressure to abolish slavery, Pedro II was unwilling to antagonise the plantation owners. The eventual abolition of slavery in 1888 was followed by the overthrow of the monarchy the next year. The Republic of Brazil was proclaimed in 1889.

Pedro II (1825–91) became emperor of Brazil at the age of five, and reigned for 58 years. His reign saw the start of industrialization in the country.

declared the creation of the United Kingdom of Portugal and Brazil, meaning that Brazil was no longer a colony. Even after the final defeat of Napoleon in 1815, Dom João stayed in Brazil, becoming king in 1816. He was forced to return to Portugal in 1821, but he left behind his son Dom Pedro as ruler in his place. When the government in Portugal tried to reduce Brazil's status back to that of a colony, Dom Pedro declared independence, on 7 September 1822. Later that year Dom Pedro was crowned emperor of Brazil.

Empire to republic

The rule of Pedro I was a time of uprising and revolt. In 1831, Pedro I abdicated, leaving the throne to his five-year-old son. It was not until 1840, when the boy was just 14, that he formally took power. The reign of Pedro II saw great advances and prosperity in Brazil. Coffee replaced sugar as the main crop, and coffee barons became

Coffee and cattle

From the last decade of the nineteenth century, immigrants from Italy, Germany, Spain, Japan and elsewhere poured into Brazil to work on the coffee plantations and in Brazil's rapidly growing cities. During this time, the new republic was dominated by two powerful sets of landowners – the coffee barons of São Paulo and the cattle ranchers of Minas Gerais. The Wall Street crash in 1929 saw the end of this era, as coffee prices tumbled and Brazil was plunged into political and economic chaos. In 1930, backed by the military, Getúlio Vargas seized power.

Getúlio Vargas

Vargas created a social welfare system in Brazil and legalized workers' unions. After 1937, however, he increasingly ruled as a dictator, imprisoning his opponents and censoring the press. His rule lasted until 1945, when he was deposed in a coup, but he was re-elected again in 1951. Faced with criticism of his government, and accusations of corruption, Vargas shot himself in 1954.

FOCUS: THE RUBBER BOOM

During the 1890s another commodity, rubber, brought huge wealth to the Amazonian cities of Belém and Manaus. With the invention of the automobile and the demand for tyres, the price of rubber rose rapidly. The Brazilian rubber boom came to an abrupt end, however, when rubber from British plantations established in southeast Asia came on to the world market in 1910, and the price dropped dramatically.

President Getúlio Vargas (centre) inspects a troop transport ship in the 1940s. Vargas sided with the Allies in World War II.

Vargas's successor, Juscelino Kubitschek, promised rapid economic expansion for Brazil and was elected on the slogan '50 years of progress in five'. Kubitschek is best remembered for the construction of Brasília, which became the country's new capital in 1960. In 1964, the presidency was overthrown in a coup and a military regime was installed.

Military rule

During the late 1960s and early 1970s the Brazilian economy boomed. The military government favoured huge projects such as the construction of a highway through the Amazon rainforest (the Trans-Amazonian highway). However, the government did nothing to address the problems of unequal land ownership (see page 19), preferring instead to concentrate on the resettlement of people in the rainforest regions. With no land on which to make a living, millions

Brasília was planned and constructed in the late 1950s to be a new capital city for Brazil. Most of the buildings were designed by the renowned Brazilian modernist architect Oscar Niemeyer.

of people began to leave rural areas for the cities. They lived in hastily built slums, called *favelas*.

The military regime was repressive. Opponents of the regime were imprisoned, tortured and often murdered. Newspapers and other media were state controlled. Unions were banned, but in the late 1970s a series of strikes began in São Paulo in opposition to the regime. Led by a factory worker called Luis Inácio da Silva (Lula for short), the strikes had widespread support. The car industry was so important to the Brazilian economy, and the support for democracy so powerful, that the military regime began to introduce reform. The country returned to civilian rule in 1985.

CHAPTER 3

Social Changes

Brazil has the fifth largest population in the world (after China, India, the United States and Indonesia). Its population is relatively young, and the average population density is low – 23 people per sq km (compared to 250 people per sq km in the United Kingdom). However, the population is very unevenly spread. The vast majority of Brazil's inhabitants live in the southeast, while the northeast and the Amazon rainforest are sparsely populated. Brazil's biggest city, São Paulo, has a population of nearly 18 million, while Rio de Janeiro has nearly 11 million inhabitants.

The *favelas*

From the 1950s to the 1970s, millions of people moved from rural areas into Brazil's cities. They came in search of work as Brazil became increasingly industrialized. With nowhere to live, most ended up in shanty towns called *favelas*, built on the edges of cities. In Rio de Janeiro, the *favelas* cling precariously to steep hillsides because of the hazard from flooding in the valleys. Landslides are an ever-present danger. As these shanty towns were built illegally they had no access to water, electricity or other services such as health or education.

Residents of Rocinha, the biggest *favela* in Brazil, walk across a bridge. You can see the buildings of the *favela* on the steep hillside in the background.

Street children, playing on a bus in Rio de Janeiro are moved on by a policeman. In Brazil, street children routinely suffer from malnutrition and disease, and often face imprisonment.

During the 1970s, the military government attempted to deal with the *favelas* by knocking them down and evicting their inhabitants. More recently, many *favela* communities have worked together to improve their circumstances. For example, in Rocinha, Rio de Janeiro, Brazil's largest *favela*, sewers and a proper water supply have been installed. However, the overcrowding and unsanitary conditions that still exist in many *favelas* are major causes of disease. Violence is another big problem, as many of these places are under the control of heavily armed gangs of drug-traffickers. Battles between rival gangs, or between drug gangs and the police, are frequently fought on the streets of the *favelas*.

Street children

Estimates of the numbers of children living on the streets of Brazil's cities range from hundreds of thousands to several million.

POPULATION

Total population: 198,739,269

Age	Percentage of population
1–14 years	26.7
15–64 years	66.8
65 years and over	6.4

Population density: 23 people per sq km
Urban population: 86% of population
Rate of urbanization: 1.8% annually (2005-10)

Source: CIA World Factbook

These children may have run away from broken homes, or lost their families to violence or disease. Many live on scraps found in rubbish bins or refuse tips. Some work on the streets, for example selling goods or as shoeshiners. Many take drugs and are involved in drug trafficking.

Because these children became involved in crime and drugs, they often become the targets of death squads. In 1993, there was worldwide outrage when eight street children were killed while sleeping outside a church in Rio de Janeiro. The members of the death squads have usually been serving in the police force or are ex-police officers. Few have ever been brought to justice.

This photograph shows a typical street in the dry northeast *sertão* of Brazil. President Lula's government has been working hard to reduce poverty in the country.

Social inequality

The problems of poverty and violence faced by Brazil have their roots in the huge gap between rich and poor. Brazil has one of the biggest income inequalities of any country in the world, with the richest 10 per cent receiving around half of the country's income, and the poorest 10 per cent receiving less than 1 per cent. In Brazil's big cities the richest and poorest often live side by side, with slum areas built next to the skyscraper homes of the wealthy. In Rio de Janeiro, a controversial plan to build walls around many *favelas* to prevent their expansion began in 2009. While officials say the walls are to prevent further destruction of the surrounding Atlantic rainforest, many people believe they are designed to separate Rio's poor from its wealthy inhabitants.

Zero Hunger

Since taking office in 2002, President Lula has put several policies in place to try to tackle social inequality and poverty. In 2003 he announced the *Fome Zero* (Zero Hunger) programme, which was designed to eradicate extreme hunger and poverty in Brazil. It was estimated that lack of money to buy enough food affected 9.3 million households; about 44 million people. Around half of these households were located in the poor northeast of the country.

Through the *bolsa familia* (family grant) scheme, money has been paid directly to mothers, depending on the level of poverty of the family and the number of children the family has in school. For many families, the money has been a lifeline and the percentage of Brazil's population

CASE STUDY: INDIAN LAND RIGHTS

Some of the most bitter and violent fights over land have been in the Amazon rainforest. Disputes are frequent between the native peoples and those who wish to exploit the rainforest for their own purposes, including loggers, miners, farmers, settlers, road- and dam-builders. Today, around 22 per cent of Brazil's Amazon territory is reserved for use by native peoples. There are still many tribes that live there with little or no contact with the outside world.

Just 3 per cent of Brazil's population owns approximately 66 per cent of all the farmland. Millions of Brazil's inhabitants do not have any land to cultivate, and millions more are squeezed onto family smallholdings. Struggles to gain access to land saw the founding of the Landless Worker's Movement (MST) in 1984. From 1985, under the slogan 'Occupy, Produce and Resist!' the MST has occupied and established farming communities on unused land. The MST claims a legal basis for these occupations in the Brazilian constitution, which states that unproductive land should be used for a 'larger social function'.

living below the poverty line dropped from 34 per cent to 25 per cent between 2003 and 2006.

Land ownership

Part of the income inequality that is a feature of life in Brazil is the issue of land ownership.

This MST march took place in Brasília in 2007. The banner reads 'For an agrarian popular reform', referring to government plans for progammes to improve life for the rural poor.

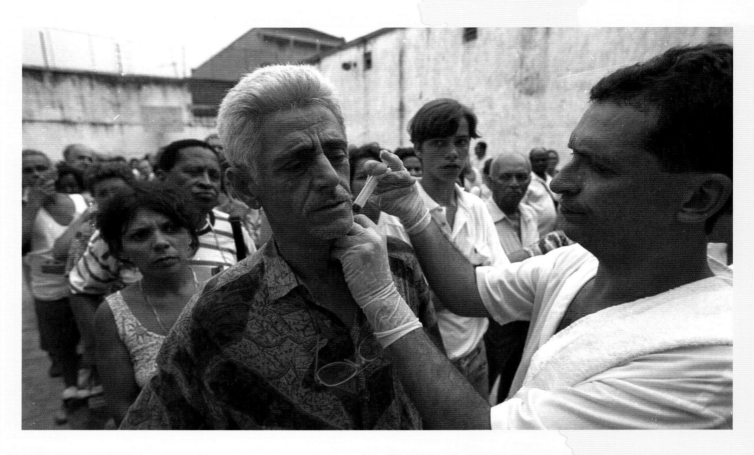

The health system

Brazil's public health system was established in the 1988 constitution and provides access to health care for all citizens. In practice, the distribution of doctors and hospitals is highest in urban areas, and lowest in the poorer, rural regions of the north and northeast. Many people who can afford it have private health care insurance.

Malaria

Factors such as climate and poverty have a major impact on people's health. Malaria is a particular problem in the Amazon region – Brazil, for example, had 40 per cent of the total number of malaria cases in the Americas in 2002. One problem is the emergence of strains of malaria that are resistant to widely-used anti-malaria drugs. Since the late 1990s, Brazil has worked closely with the World Health Organization and other Latin American countries to collect information about the spread

Brazil has a national immunization programme that targets children, teenagers and adults. Here, 300 people wait in line to receive a vaccination.

of malaria, and the effectiveness of various drugs.

Living with HIV

In 2007, Brazil had roughly 730,000 people living with HIV, about 0.6 per cent of the adult population. This was just over half the number that had been estimated in a government report of the previous decade. Brazil's achievement in fighting AIDS is seen as a major success story. Brazil introduced the provision of free antiretroviral drugs for people with HIV in 1991, and it has consistently put pressure on the major drug companies to lower the costs of these drugs. The Brazilian government has calculated that as a result of its policies the number of people dying of AIDS-related illnesses has dropped by 50 per cent since the late 1990s.

COMPARING COUNTRIES – HIV/AIDS

Country	Living with HIV/AIDS		Deaths due to AIDS during 2007
	All people	Adult (15-49) rate %	
Argentina	120,000	0.5	5,400
Belize	3,600	2.1	<200
Bolivia	8,100	0.2	<500
Brazil	730,000	0.6	15,000
Chile	31,000	0.3	<1,000
Colombia	170,000	0.6	9,800
Costa Rica	9,700	0.4	<200
Ecuador	26,000	0.3	1,200
El Salvador	35,000	0.8	1,700
Guatemala	59,000	0.8	3,900
Guyana	13,000	2.5	<1,000
Honduras	28,000	0.7	1,800
Mexico	200,000	0.3	11,000
Nicaragua	7,700	0.2	<500
Panama	20,000	1.0	<1,000
Paraguay	21,000	0.6	<1,000
Peru	76,000	0.5	3,300
Suriname	6,800	2.4	–
Uruguay	10,000	0.6	<500
Venezuela	–	–	–
Total	1,700,000	0.5	63,000

Source: www.avert.org/southamerica.htm   Note: < = less than

Education

Education in Brazil is free and compulsory for primary school children (ages 7 to 14), and free but not compulsory for secondary school (ages 15 to 17). Schools in the wealthier states of the south and southeast are much better funded, with more facilities and teachers than those of the poorer north and northeastern regions. Although the average adult rate of literacy for Brazil is 91 per cent, the percentage of people who are illiterate is as high as 20 per cent in the northeast.

Even though primary education is free, many children from poor families do not attend because their families need them to work and earn money. In recent years, this situation has improved thanks to the *bolsa escola* (school grant), which rewards parents in poor families who keep their children in school (95 per cent attendance in 2007). Nevertheless, critics of President Lula accuse his government of not doing enough to improve educational standards, which they see as vital to help lift communities, particularly in deprived rural areas, out of poverty.

This is a rural school in the Amazon region of Brazil. Today, better education is seen as vital to help reduce poverty in the country.

Murder and corruption

Brazil has a reputation for violence in its cities. The murder rate more than doubled between 1980 and 2002, from 11.4 deaths for every 100,000 people to 28 deaths per 100,000. In 2000, Brazil had a murder rate nearly four times higher than that of the United States. Murder is still the major cause of death for people between the ages of 15 and 44 in Brazil. There are several factors that contribute to the violence that blights many of Brazil's cities – income inequality and poverty in a large percentage of the population, the drug culture in many of the *favelas*, and police corruption.

These prisoners are protesting in their compound. Their banners read 'PCC for justice and liberty' and 'Against oppression'. The PCC is one of several powerful gangs that operate out of Brazil's prisons.

INCOME INEQUALITY COMPARISON

Share of national household income 1995-2005

Brazil
Lowest 40% of population received 9%
Highest 20% of population received 61%

United States
Lowest 40% of population received 16%
Highest 20% of population received 46%

United Kingdom
Lowest 40% of population received 18%
Highest 20% of population received 44%

Gang violence

In May 2006, a wave of violence overwhelmed São Paulo and more than 150 people died in a

series of attacks on buses, banks and police stations. The violence was organized by a prison gang called the First Command of the Capital (PCC). The PCC is one of several prison gangs that work from inside Brazil's jails, and which are involved in drug trafficking, kidnapping, robberies and prison riots. Gang leaders are able to communicate with the outside world by mobile phones that are smuggled in, often with the help of corrupt prison guards. In response to the violence in May 2006, the police killed 100 so-called 'suspects'.

Brazil's prisons

The violence in 2006 was sparked by the movement of hundreds of PCC prisoners to higher-security jails. Brazil's prison system is so overcrowded that prisoners are often held in appalling conditions. Each state runs its own prisons, although the government has begun the construction of high-security federal prisons as

Here armed police are at work in the Engenho da Rainha *favela* in Rio de Janeiro, checking for drugs and guns. Drug gangs are a major problem in many *favelas*.

part of its strategy to deal with the gang violence. The first of these, Cantanduva Federal Penitentiary in Parana state, opened in 2006.

Tackling the drug gangs

In 2008, the police launched a new approach to dealing with drug gangs in Rio de Janeiro. Instead of raiding a *favela* and then withdrawing, as had been the pattern in the past, the police aim to maintain a round-the-clock presence. This plan has been put into action in the Santa Marta *favela*, and community policing is being backed up by government money to improve living conditions. But even if this new approach is a success in Santa Marta, critics point out that the cost of policing every *favela* in this way will be enormous.

CHAPTER 4

Political Changes

Brazil's return to civilian rule in 1985 (see page 15) did not go smoothly. The elected president, Tancredo Neves, died before he could take office, so his place was taken by the vice-president, José Sarney. During Sarney's time in office, Brazil's economy slumped and the country accumulated a massive foreign debt. In 1989, the presidential election was won by Fernando Collor de Mello, who beat the leader of the Workers' Party, Luis ('Lula') Inácio da Silva, by a small margin. Collor, however, was forced to resign in 1992, after a corruption scandal.

Fernando Henrique Cardoso

As Brazil's inflation rate soared, the government introduced the Real Plan, introducing a new currency called the *real* and severely limiting government spending. The success of the plan saw the man who had devised it, Fernando Henrique Cardoso, become Brazil's next president in 1994. Once again, Lula lost the election – this time by a large margin. Cardoso was a popular president, and he oversaw the country's return to a stable economy. He was re-elected for a second term in 1998. Having served two terms, the constitution did not permit Cardoso to stand for election again in 2002. Lula won this election with 61 per cent of the national vote.

President Cardoso addresses an audience on an official visit to Chile in 2002. He was president of Brazil for eight years (1994–2002).

President Lula (centre with hands raised) makes a point at a meeting with heads of Latin American and Caribbean countries in 2008.

President Lula

Lula was Brazil's first president to come from a left-wing background. Some people were worried that his policies would send the country's economy into a downturn, but Lula continued with the strict measures that were keeping inflation under control, and paid off the country's foreign debt. At the same time he turned his attention to the country's poor. He introduced the *bolsa familia* (family grant; see page 18), as well as some land reforms. Despite corruption scandals that rocked his Workers' Party in 2005 and 2006, he was elected for a second term in 2006.

Lula is an immensely popular president in Brazil, but his government continues to face major challenges, including education and the ongoing issues of land reform. The biggest challenge of all remains the huge inequality between rich and poor.

CASE STUDY: LULA (1945–)

Luis ('Lula') Inácio da Silva was born in Pernacumbo state in the northeast into a poor family. He worked as a street vendor, a shoeshine boy and a delivery boy to bring in money for his family. In 1966, he found work in a metalwork factory in São Paulo, where he became involved in the union movement. He led the strikes of the late 1970s that helped to remove the military regime, and in 1980 he was one of the founders of the Workers' Party (PT). He was imprisoned for 31 days for his political activities in 1980. He became president of Brazil at his fourth attempt in 2002.

Political parties

In 1979, the first steps towards democracy were taken when the military government allowed the formation of new political parties. Since then there have been numerous small parties on the Brazilian political scene, with about 20 represented in the Chamber of Deputies, Brazil's parliament. However, there are four main parties: the Workers' Party (PT), the Brazilian Social Democratic Party (PSDB), the Party of the Brazilian Democratic Movement (PMDB) and Democratas (Dem). The PT is a left-wing party born out of the union strikes of the late 1970s (see page 15). The PMDB is a centre party, while the PSDB was formed in the late 1980s out of the PMDB by Cardoso and others, and is particularly popular with Brazil's middle classes. Democratas is a conservative, right-wing party that strongly opposes the government of the PT.

Brazil's government

Brazil is a federative republic. It is divided into 26 states and a Federal District that includes the capital city, Brasília. The states and the Federal District each has its own government. Every state has its own constitution and its own judiciary system. The states themselves are divided into more than 5,000 municipalities, each of which has its own elected mayor.

The president of Brazil is directly elected by the people every four years. A president may serve two terms. He or she controls the country's budget and has the power to introduce, amend

This photograph shows the National Congress building in Brasília. The upturned 'dish-shaped' building houses the Federal Senate. The Chamber of Deputies meets in the domed building.

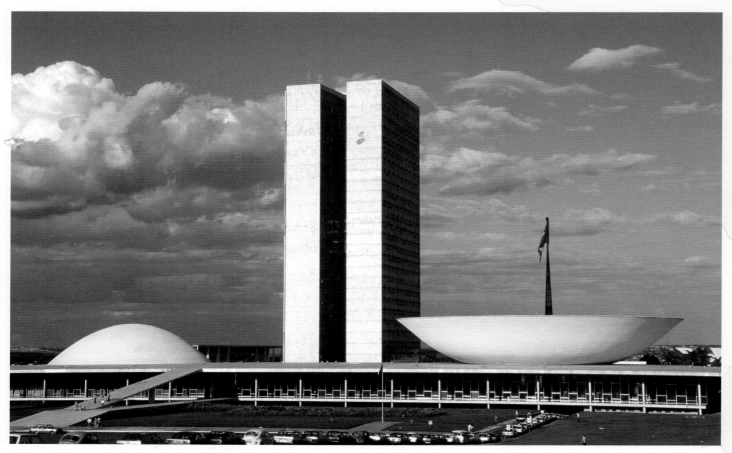

Federative Republic of Brazil

Executive and Legislative

- **President** (Head of State and Head of Federal Government)
- **Vice-President Ministers**
- **National Congress**
  - **Federal Senate** (81 members)
  - **Chamber of Deputies** (513 members)
- **26 states and 1 Federal District** each with own government and judicial system
- **5,000 municipalities** each with an elected mayor

Judicial Supreme Court

- **State** (26 Courts of Justice)
- **Federal** (5 regional Federal Courts)

Brazil has a federal government. The president is both Head of State and Head of the Federal Government.

and veto legislation, as well as promoting relationships and treaties with other states. The president works with the National Congress which has two houses – the Federal Senate and the Chamber of Deputies. The Federal Senate has 81 members, three from every state and the Federal District, who are elected for an eight-year term. The Chamber of Deputies has 513 members who are elected from each state and the Federal District for a four-year term.

The constitution

Since gaining independence in 1822, Brazil has had eight constitutions. The last one, passed in 1988, abolished the restrictive laws laid down by the military regime. It defined the civil rights of the individual, set the minimum voting age at 16, restricted the president's powers, and set out the organization of the state. It has been amended since 1988, but its fundamental principles remain the same.

CASE STUDY: PRESS FREEDOM

The 1988 constitution guarantees the freedom of the media to work without any censorship. However some laws remained in place from the military era that threatened freedom of speech in Brazil. In 2009, a court voted to remove a law that could be used to imprison journalists for crimes such as libel or slander. There are hundreds of newspapers and television channels that report freely in Brazil. Yet journalists who try to investigate ongoing problems such as political corruption, poverty or drug trafficking can face danger both from criminal gangs, and from law enforcers.

CHAPTER 5

Economic Changes

Brazil has the tenth largest economy in the world. It has well-developed agribusiness, mining, manufacturing and service sectors. At various times in the past, Brazil dominated world trade in sugar, coffee and rubber. Today, agriculture remains very important for the country's economy. Most commercial crops are grown in the south and southeast, and they include coffee, soybeans, oranges, sugar cane, cacao, cotton and rice. Animal feed products, made from soybeans, are a major export, and Brazil is the world's biggest exporter of orange juice. Cattle ranching is also big business in southern and central Brazil, making the country one of the world's biggest meat exporters. However, the expansion of cattle ranching into rainforest areas is a major cause of deforestation (see pages 33 and 34).

A food superpower?

It is likely that agriculture will continue to expand in Brazil. Of the 350 million hectares of land available for agriculture, only between 70 and 80 million are currently being exploited. With the

A worker at the Conquista farm in Alfenas, Minas Gerais, inspects coffee beans which are drying in the sun. This farm belongs to Ipanema Coffee, one of the largest speciality coffee companies in the world.

Huge trucks transport iron ore at the Carajas mine in the state of Para. This mine has over 1.5 billion tons of iron ore reserves.

BRIC

Brazil is one of four countries identified by economists as having such potential, they could be the four most dominant economies in the world by 2050. Known as BRIC, the countries are Brazil, Russia, India and China. Although BRIC is not a formal trading alliance or economic organization, representatives from the four BRIC countries have held meetings to discuss matters such as finance, security and the fight against drug trafficking.

continuing growth in world population, there is huge potential for Brazil to become a food superpower. There are concerns, however, about the effects of the drive to grow more crops on environments such as the *cerrado* and the rainforests. Another issue is poor infrastructure in many regions, particularly roads and ports, which makes the transportation of goods difficult and costly. The government has recently approved several projects to build and upgrade roads, including a new highway to link São Paulo and Rio de Janeiro.

Industry and mining

Industry and mining is concentrated in the south and southeast regions. There are large natural reserves of minerals including nickel, tin, chromite and uranium, as well as gold and precious and semiprecious stones. Brazil's manufacturing industries include motor vehicles and parts, electrical machinery, aircraft, computers, chemicals, textiles and shoes. Many industries are located in São Paulo state, which produces more than half of the goods manufactured in Brazil.

COMPARING COUNTRIES – ECONOMY

	Brazil	India
GDP growth rate (2008 est.)	5.2%	6.6%
GDP per capita (2008 est.)	$10,100	$2,800
GDP by sector:		
agriculture	5.5%	17.2%
industry	28.5%	29.1%
services (2008 est.)	66%	53.7%
Labour force by occupation:		
agriculture	20%	60%
industry	14%	12%
services (2003 est.)	66%	12%
Unemployment (2008)	8%	6.8%

Source: CIA World Factbook

29

Economic policies

Brazil has plentiful natural resources, including recently discovered oil reserves, and a healthy economy. When President Lula took office in 2003, he largely continued with the economic policies of his predecessor, stabilizing the Brazilian economy and paying off foreign debt. After his re-election in 2006, he introduced the Accelerated Growth Program. This US $240 billion, four-year plan is designed to boost economic growth though investment. It includes plans to restructure Brazil's tax system, and to modernize the country's road and rail system.

Since 2003, Brazil's economy has benefited from high world prices for commodities such as coffee, soybeans and iron ore. However, the global recession that started in 2008 caused prices to tumble and slowed down the growth of Brazil's economy. Nevertheless, most economists still think that Brazil is well placed to weather the global financial crisis.

Employment

In 2008, unemployment in Brazil stood at around 8 per cent. The global recession hit industries such as steel and vehicle manufacture, as well as the mining industry. The unemployment rate was higher in the less-developed and poorer regions of the northeast. However, the government expected the country to recover rapidly from the effects of the recession. More long-term problems that remain are those of job instability and poor working conditions. More than one-third of people in work are in temporary jobs. Examples include jobs in tourist resorts, or harvesting crops such as sugar cane or tobacco. Thousands of people are migrant workers, moving to different parts of the country to find seasonal work. In many cases these people work long hours for low pay – some in atrocious conditions.

Boa Viagem beach in Recife is protected by a line of natural reefs which form pools as the tide goes out. The city is a popular tourist destination.

WORLD ETHANOL PRODUCTION

Country	Millions of gallons
United States	6,498.6
Brazil	5,019.2
European Union	570.3
China	486.0
Canada	211.3
Thailand	79.2
Columbia	74.9
India	52.8
Central America	39.6
Australia	26.4
Turkey	15.8
Pakistan	9.2
Peru	7.9
Argentina	5.2
Paraguay	4.7
Total	**13,101.1**

Source: Ethanol World Production Statistics, 2008 (www.ethanol.net)

An ethanol plant in São Paulo. Brazil has invested heavily in ethanol production since the 1970s as a greener alternative to petrol.

Ethanol

Brazil is the tenth largest energy consumer in the world, and its energy consumption has increased rapidly in recent years. The country became energy independent in 2006, and 46 per cent of Brazil's energy production is from renewable resources, making it one of the greenest countries in the world. Since the 1970s, Brazil has invested in ethanol, a plant-based fuel made from sugar cane. All petrol in Brazil contains ethanol, and half of all the cars in the country are flexi-fuel, which means they can run on petrol or ethanol. The production of ethanol has made Brazil less reliant on oil, and ethanol is exported to countries such as Japan and Sweden.

CHAPTER 6

Environmental Changes

The rainforest that covers almost all of northern Brazil is one of the wonders of the world. It is home to around 30 per cent of all known species on our planet, as well as many thousands of species that are yet to be identified. Its biodiversity is astounding: one hectare of rainforest may contain more than 480 species of trees, and some 1,800 butterflies have been described (compared to the 321 known species in Europe).

There are many reasons why the rainforest is important not only for the people who live there, but for everyone on the planet. Its biodiversity is a vital source of food, chemicals and medicines – roughly one-quarter of medicines used in the developed world have their origins in rainforest materials. The rainforests are also huge carbon dioxide stores, and when forests are burned to clear land the carbon dioxide is released into the atmosphere, adding to global warming.

Developing the rainforest

The development of the rainforest began in the 1940s, but farmers found that crops did not grow in the poor rainforest soils. Cattle ranchers had more success on the cleared rainforest land. However, development was fairly limited until the 1970s, when the military government in Brazil launched a plan to move people into rainforest areas from the poor regions of the northeast. As part of the plan, the government started the

Blue-and-yellow macaws are just one of the many colourful birds that can be seen in Brazil's rainforest regions. There are over 1,000 species of birds including toucans, macaws, hoatzins and the rare harpy eagle.

Causes of deforestation in the Amazon

Logging 4%

Fires 4%

Large scale agriculture 2%

Subsistence farming 30%

Cattle ranches 60%

Source: www.mongabay.com

Cattle ranching is the leading cause of deforestation in the Amazon rainforest. It accounts for more than half of the trees destroyed in the area.

of the rainforest, often on neighbouring *cerrado* or on areas that have already been cleared, it has the effect of pushing cattle ranchers and other farmers even further into the rainforest. It also encourages the construction of new roads, which attracts poor farmers, loggers and others to settle and move onto rainforest land.

construction of the 3,000-km Trans-Amazonian highway, opening up the interior of the rainforest to settlers, cattle ranchers, miners and loggers.

The scheme to settle in the rainforest was a failure – the soils were quickly exhausted, and many settlers left their plots and moved to Brazil's rapidly expanding cities. The abandoned land was taken up by cattle ranchers, who cleared yet more land for their herds. Cattle ranching has remained the single biggest cause of deforestation since the 1970s, as the world demand for meat has risen and Brazil has increased its production.

Soybean cultivation

More recently, the cultivation of soybeans has become a factor in deforestation. Brazil has become one of the world's leading exporters of soybeans, which are used for cattle feed and oil. Although most soybean cultivation is on the edge

Areas of rainforest are cleared by 'slash and burn'. This is a method where vegetation is cut down and then burned to clear the ground. As a result, the exposed soils are quickly exhausted.

A logging truck carries a load of logs on a dirt road. Illegal logging remains a major problem in Brazil. Once the forest has been cleared, land may be cultivated or used to graze cattle. However Amazon land is not fertile: after one harvest, the land is no longer arable, so more land must be cleared by burning or logging.

The government, however, has attributed drops in the deforestation rate from 2005 onwards to better monitoring and control. For example, all logging activity in the rainforest requires a licence, but illegal logging continues to be a major problem. Aside from the damage caused by removing trees, the tracks used by the loggers to remove the wood open up new areas of forest, allowing farmers and ranchers to move in. Since 2003, the Brazilian Federal Environment Agency, (IBAMA), has had some success in tracking and breaking up several large gangs involved in illegal logging activities. In 2006, Lula announced plans for sustainable logging schemes that will limit the damage done to the forest, and provide more income for local people.

Deforestation

Since 1970, around 600,000 sq km of rainforest have been destroyed in Brazil. The rate of deforestation has been strongly linked to the country's economic performance – at times of economic growth demand for rainforest products, such as timber, has increased, while during difficult economic times the clearance has slowed.

Protected land

Other measures to protect the rainforest include increasing the amount of federally protected land.

FOCUS: HYDROELECTRIC PROJECTS

Brazil generates 84 per cent of its electricity from hydroelectric schemes. While hydroelectricity is both clean and renewable (unlike electricity generated from coal-powered power stations, for example), the construction of large dams raises many environmental issues. To meet Brazil's increasing demand for power, the government is set to build two dams on the Madeira river in the Amazon state of Rondonia. The dams are due for completion by 2012. Critics of the scheme warn that rotting vegetation in the reservoir created by the dam will release greenhouse gases, and that the dams will block migratory routes for several fish species in the river.

A balancing act

The Brazilian government constantly has to balance plans for economic development against environmental concerns. One example is Highway BR-163, a 1,770 km-long road that cuts across the Amazon rainforest from Santarém to Cuiaba in the northern state of Pará. Most of the highway is unpaved, meaning that travel is slow, and during the rainy season it can become so muddy that no vehicles can use it at all. The government has plans to pave the entire road, to improve access for soybean cultivation. But past experience has shown that improving access opens up the rainforest to exploitation. In response to these concerns, the government has created seven new protected areas along the route of the road.

The ten-year Amazon Region Protected Areas (ARPA) Program was launched in 2002, with the aim of bringing one-third of all Amazon rainforest into protected status. In the same year the Tumucumaque National Park was created, covering an area of unspoilt rainforest that is bigger than Belgium. Since then, Lula's government has created 57 protected areas in the Amazon, covering around 195,000 sq km.

This is a dam on the Tocantins River in Goais state. The construction of dams on Brazil's rivers is a controversial issue in the country.

Atlantic rainforest

Worldwide concern about deforestation in the Amazon rainforest can overshadow environmental issues elsewhere in Brazil. The country's amazing biodiversity is equally as rich in other regions, for example the Atlantic rainforest, or the Pantanal, and there are pressing environmental problems in these areas too.

Less than 10 per cent of the original Atlantic rainforest remains, and even this area is under extreme pressure from the expansion of cities, and from farmland. Out of 20,000 plant species, 40 per cent are found only in the Atlantic rainforest. There are also 72 species of mammal and 144 species of bird that live only in these regions. The mammals include the endangered lion tamarins, and muriquis – also known as woolly spider monkeys. In Brazil, about 24,000 sq km of Atlantic rainforest is strictly protected as national and state parks. Many areas of Atlantic rainforest tend to be small fragments, so priority has been given to establishing 'conservation corridors' to link the fragments together. Working closely with the people who live on this land, the aim is to reforest these corridors, or to encourage land use compatible with the rainforest environment.

The Pantanal

The world's largest freshwater wetland, the Pantanal is flooded every year by the waters of the Paraguay river. During the wet season the swamp is home to 260 species of fish; in the dry season it attracts vast numbers of birds. It is also

During the dry season, the flood waters recede in the Pantanal, leaving numerous beautiful blue lagoons surrounded by lush vegetation.

Baby hawksbill sea turtles make their way across Forte beach to the ocean in the state of Bahia. This beach is protected by Project Tamar.

home to jaguars, giant otters, giant anteaters and brightly coloured hyacinth macaws. Threats to this region arise mainly from economic development in and around the Pantanal. For example, fertilizers and herbicides used on the crops grown on Brazil's central plain run into the streams and rivers that feed the Pantanal. Pollution from inadequate sewage systems in the region's cities also ends up in the swamp.

The *cerrado*

More than half of the vast area of grassland, called *cerrado*, that covers Brazil's central plateau has disappeared during the last 40 years. The *cerrado* has many unique plant species, as well as being home to mammals such as the maned wolf, the giant armadillo and the Brazilian tapir. The founding of Brasília in the 1950s (see page 15) was designed to encourage settlement in the interior of the country. The construction of roads allowed cattle and agricultural products to be easily transported out of the region, and it quickly became a centre of agribusiness. Today 58 per cent of Brazil's soybean crop is grown in the

cerrado region, and there are nearly 40 million cattle on its ranches. Only a small area of the *cerrado* is protected, and its potential for the expansion of agribusiness means that it is unlikely to receive the levels of conservation given to the rainforest areas.

CASE STUDY: PROJECT TAMAR

Project Tamar was set up in 1980 to protect sea turtles along the country's coastline. Turtle numbers were declining rapidly as a result of poaching, fishing, and the collecting of eggs on beaches. Since 1980, Project Tamar has worked closely with local fishing communities to protect the turtles, particularly during the nesting season. A vital part of the project's success has been to involve local people – often former poachers – and to help communities find alternative sources of income to replace the exploitation of the turtles.

CHAPTER 7

Changing Relationships

Brazil is increasingly emerging as a global power. Under the leadership of President Lula, Brazil has particularly engaged with other countries that have rapidly developing economies, notably India, China, South Africa and Russia. President Lula has also strengthened relationships with the other South American countries, and with many less-developed countries in Africa.

Trading partners

Brazil's major trading partners are the United States, China, Argentina and Germany. Since the 1930s, the United States has been Brazil's biggest trade partner for both imports and exports. However, in May 2009, a surge in Chinese demand for Brazilian iron ore pushed China ahead of the United States as Brazil's leading trading partner. It marked the increasing importance of China as a market for Brazil and other South American countries. Brazilian exports to China are largely made up of soybeans, iron ore and fuel, and deals to export oil are likely.

G-20 developing countries

Brazil is a member of the G-20, a group of 23 developing countries from around the world. The G-20 focuses on agricultural issues, and was established just before a meeting of the World

This photograph shows a container port in Rio de Janeiro. Foreign trade is vitally important to Brazil's economy.

The president of Paraguay speaks at a ceremony in celebration of the 18th anniversary of the founding of Mercosur in 2009.

Bolivia, Chile, Colombia, Ecuador and Peru are associate members. The purpose of the trading bloc is to encourage the free movement of goods and people between member countries. There has, however, been a history of disagreements within Mercosur, for example in 1999 when Argentina imposed tariffs on steel imports from Brazil. The issue was resolved in 2000, but arguments between members persist. In particular, Paraguay and Uruguay complain that Brazil and Argentina, which between them account for 95 per cent of the Gross Domestic Product (GDP) of Mercosur, have too much power in the organization.

Trade Organization (WTO) that was held in Cancún, Mexico, in 2003. The G-20 objected to proposals from the United States and the countries of the European Union that, under WTO rules, developing countries should reduce tariffs and open their markets to agricultural imports. Brazil and other countries argued that the rules were unfair because of subsidies in the US and the European Union that would allow farmers there to flood the markets with cheap imports. As a result of the G-20 intervention, the WTO talks collapsed. Negotiations are still underway to try to reach an agreement between all the member countries.

Mercosur

Another important trade grouping is Mercosur. Often called the Common Market of the South, this trade bloc was set up in 1991 by Argentina, Brazil, Paraguay and Uruguay. The membership of Venezuela has yet to be fully agreed, and

EXPORT AND IMPORT PARTNERS (2007)

Country	Exports	Imports
United States	16.1%	15.7%
Argentina	9.2%	8.6%
China	6.8%	10.5%
Netherlands	5.6%	
Germany	4.6%	7.2%
Nigeria		4.4%

Source: CIA World Factbook

Brazilian President Lula (right) met the new US president, Barack Obama (left), at the White House in Washington DC in March 2009.

Brazil and the United States

While the relationship between Brazil and the United States is an important one, President Lula was not afraid to criticize some of the policies of George W. Bush. Brazil was an outspoken critic of the US-led war on Iraq, for example. Both countries are major producers of ethanol – between them they supply about 70 per cent of the world market. However, while Brazil has many decades of experience of producing ethanol from sugar cane, the United States makes its ethanol from corn (maize). Corn-based ethanol is more expensive to produce and takes up high-grade land that could be used for food crops. Lula has spoken out against the subsidies given by the United States to its farmers to grow corn for ethanol,

UNASUR

In May 2008, a treaty was signed in Brasília to create the Union of South American Nations (UNASUR). Members of UNASUR are Argentina, Bolivia, Brazil, Chile, Colombia, Ecuador, Guyana, Paraguay, Peru, Suriname, Uruguay and Venezuela. The intention is to create an organization like the European Union, with its own parliament, bank and currency. However, critics say that political and economic integration of the region will be difficult because there are serious differences between some of its members.

CASE STUDY: OIL DISCOVERIES

Brazil has the second-largest oil reserves in South America, after Venezuela. Almost all of the oil production is controlled by Petrobras, and the main region for production is Rio de Janeiro state. In 2007, Petrobras announced that it had discovered new reserves of oil in an offshore oilfield called Tupi. The oilfield is estimated to contain at least 5 to 8 billion barrels of oil, at a depth of 5,500 m below the surface of the ocean. Brazil's rising oil production means that it is likely to become an oil exporter in the near future.

and the high taxes applied to imports into the United States of cheaper sugar-based ethanol from Brazil. However, in 2007, Brazil and the United States signed an agreement to work together on the next generation of biofuels.

The election of Barack Obama as US president saw a new chapter in Brazilian-US relations. Obama has spoken of becoming a 'full partner' with the countries of Latin America, and meetings between the US president and President Lula have opened up new possibilities for issues including the economy, energy and the environment.

The United Nations

Brazil is a member of the United Nations (UN). Together with Germany, Japan and India, Brazil,

is looking for a permanent seat on the UN Security Council, which has responsibility for international peace and security. At the moment, the council has five permanent members, China, France, Russia, the United Kingdom and the United States. Ten non-permanent members are elected for a two-year term. The Brazilian army has taken part in many UN peacekeeping efforts, most recently in Haiti, where Brazil led the peacekeeping troops.

UN peacekeepers from Brazil quickly take up their positions after hearing gunshots in Port-au-Prince, the capital of Haiti, in 2006.

CHAPTER 8

Future Challenges

Brazil seems better placed than most countries to weather the global recession. It is a country abounding in natural wealth – it has the largest area of rainforest in the world, an amazing biodiversity with many untapped possibilities, huge mineral reserves and vast tracts of productive agricultural land. One of the biggest challenges is to manage this land in a sustainable way for future generations.

Sustainable development

It is vital that plans to protect the land take into account the needs of local people. Examples of successful projects include two Sustainable Development Reserves (SDR) in the Amazon, one around the Purus river near the city of Manaus, the other in Mamirauá and Amanã in central Amazonia. In both these reserves local people receive support to decide on issues such as fishing quotas, or the amount of timber that can be logged sustainably. They also patrol the region to monitor illegal activity, such as poaching, mining or logging. Projects such as this are vital to achieve both conservation and sustainable development for the future.

Inequality

The biggest challenge that affects Brazilian society as a whole remains the inequality between rich and poor. While economic growth is vital for the country, it does not address the issues that cause inequality. These issues include unequal land distribution, regional poverty and access to education. Policies such as Zero Hunger and the *bolsa familia* put in

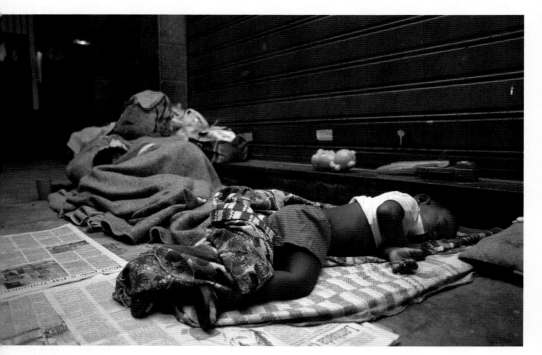

Children sleep on a pavement on a rough bed of blankets and newspapers. Such poverty is one of the biggest challenges facing Brazil's government.

Football is the national sport in Brazil and brings people together from all ethnic backgrounds and social groups. It's played everywhere; from the streets of the *favelas* to the Maracana Stadium in Rio. These players are from the Fluminense FC team.

place by President Lula's government have helped many poor families. But many people have criticised the government for not doing enough to improve education, which is acknowledged to be an important factor in reducing inequality. While government initiatives have improved the number of children attending primary school, less than half of the population completes secondary school. Free university education tends to benefit the better-off, as children from poorer homes are less likely to go on to secondary and university education.

Afro-Brazilians

Since 2003, 20 November has been Black Consciousness day in Brazil. It commemorates the slave leader Zumbi (see page 11), and celebrations are held all over Brazil. Also in 2003, the prestigious Rio de Janeiro State University announced that it would reserve a certain number of places for black students. Since then, a racial quota system has been introduced across all Brazil's universities, reserving 20 per cent of places for Afro-Brazilians. Such measures are controversial, but many people think they are necessary to address the low economic status of the black population in Brazil.

CASE STUDY: ECOTOURISM

Ecotourism is environmentally responsible tourism that promotes conservation, has a low impact on the environment and is beneficial for local people. It is increasingly a potential source of income for people in Brazil. Many ecotourism projects already exist, such as one run by Project Tamar (see page 37) and another that is linked to a project to save the muriqui (see page 36). New projects are planned for the Amazon region, where the difficulty and expense of access has so far prevented the widespread development of tourism.

Timeline

c.9,000 BCE Early peoples established in the region by this date.

1500 Pedro Alvares Cabral lands in Brazi.l

1530 Portuguese set up first colonies in Brazil.

1549 Arrival of governor-general, Tomé de Sousa. First capital established at Salvador.

1550s Establishment of sugar cane plantations and arrival of first black slaves from west Africa.

1695 Gold is discovered in Minas Gerais.

1763 Rio de Janeiro becomes the colonial capital.

1807 Portuguese royal family arrive in Portugal.

1815 Creation of the United Kingdom of Portugal and Brazil.

1820s Start of coffee boom in Brazil.

1822 Declaration of independence.

1888 Slavery is abolished in Brazil.

1890s and 1900s Large numbers of European and Japanese immigrants arrive in Brazil.

1889 Monarchy is overthrown and Republic of Brazil is proclaimed.

1930 Getúlio Vargas seizes power.

1939-45 World War II – Brazil declares itself neutral, then joins the Allies in 1943.

1945 Vargas is deposed in a coup.

1951 Vargas is elected president.

1954 Vargas commits suicide.

1956-61 Juscelino Kubitschek is president.

1960 Capital moved to Brasília.

1964 Start of military regime.

1985 Civilian rule is restored. Tancredo Neves is elected president but dies before he takes office. José Sarney becomes president.

1988 New constitution.

1989-92 Fernando Collor de Mello is president – he resigns after being accused of corruption.

1994-2002 Fernando Henrique Cardoso is president – he launches Real Plan.

2002 Luis ('Lula') Inácio da Silva wins presidential election.

2003 President Lula announces Zero Hunger programme.

2005 Corruption scandal hits Workers' Party.

2006 Lula re-elected as president. Violence and riots in São Paulo.

2008 Global recession hits Brazilian economy.

Glossary

Afro-Brazilian A Brazilian with mixed ancestry, including African, European or native Indian ancestors.

agribusiness Any business involved in the farming and food production industry.

Amerindian Indigenous people of South America. There are approximately 700,000 Amerindians in Brazil.

antiretroviral drug Any drug used to treat or suppress retroviruses, such as HIV.

bandeirantes Adventurers who explored the interior of Brazil during the seventeenth and eighteenth centuries, and who terrorized the native peoples.

biodiversity The variety of life in a particular environment.

biofuel Any fuel that is derived from biomass – organic matter such as plants.

caatinga A type of vegetation found in northeastern Brazil and characterized by hardy thorny shrubs and cacti.

Candomblé An African-Brazilian religion that is a mixture of the Catholic faith with traditional African beliefs.

cerrado The term used for the savannah grassland that covers much of the Brazilian Central Plateau.

commodity A product or good that can be sold.

constitution A written document that establishes the rules and codes of government for a particular country.

coup An overthrow of a government, often with the use of violence.

deforestation The removal of tree cover.

democracy A political system in which people vote for their government or rulers in free elections.

dictator Someone who rules with absolute and unrestricted power.

drug trafficking The process of receiving and selling on illegal drugs.

epidemic Describes an outbreak of disease that affects a large proportion of a population.

ethanol A plant-based fuel that is made from sugar cane or corn (maize).

favela A slum or shanty town in a Brazilian city.

federative republic A federation of states with a republican form of government.

global warming The process by which the average temperatures on Earth are gradually rising.

greenhouse gas Any gas that acts like a greenhouse in Earth's atmosphere by trapping energy from the sun close to the Earth's surface.

gross domestic product (GDP) A way of measuring the amount of wealth a country produces.

immunity Resistance to an infection or a disease.

inflation The overall upward price movement of goods and services in an economy.

infrastructure The structures that allow a society to function, for example roads, telecommunications, rail networks etc.

Jesuit A member of the Society of Jesus, an order of the Roman Catholic Church.

literacy The ability to read and write.

malaria An infectious disease that is common in tropcial and sub-tropical regions. It is most commonly transmitted by bites from mosquitoes which carry blood infected with the malaria parasites from person to person.

mestiço Describes a Brazilian of mixed European, native Indian or black African ancestry.

plantation A large farm or estate set up for the cultivation of cash crops.

quilombo A free community set up by escaped slaves in seventeenth century Brazil.

real Brazil's currency since 1994.

savannah Tropical grassland.

sertão The dry plains of northeastern Brazil.

sustainable The use of resources in such a way that there is no long-term damage to the natural environment.

urbanization The process of people moving from rural areas to live in urban (city) areas.

Further information

Books

Major World Leaders: Luiz Inácio Lula Da Silva by John Morrison (Chelsea House Publishers, 2005)

National Geographic Countries of the World: Brazil by Zilah Quezado Deckker (National Geographic Society, 2008)

Nations of the World: Brazil by Anita Dalal (Raintree, 2003)

Real-Life Stories: Street Child Hamilton's Story (Ticktock Media, 2005)

The Changing Face of Brazil by Edward Parker (Wayland, 2007)

Travel Through: Brazil by Joe Fullman (QED Publishing, 2007)

Visual Geography: Brazil in Pictures by Tom Streissguth (Lerner Books, 2009)

World in Focus: Brazil by Simon Scoones (Hachette, 2006)

Websites

www.brazil.org.uk/index.html
Embassy of Brazil in London website.

http://rainforests.mongabay.com/amazon/
Learn all about the Amazon rainforest.

www.iracambi.com/english/atlantic_ rainforest.shtml#mata
Information about the Atlantic rainforest.

http://news.bbc.co.uk/1/hi/world/americas/country_ profiles/1227110.stm
BBC country profile with links to news stories about Brazil.

www.brasil.gov.br/ingles/about_brazil/
Brazilian government website.

www.mstbrazil.org/?q=about
Website of the Landless Workers Movement (MST).

Index